The Tumultuous Reign of Donald the First

A Highly Partisan Cartoon History of the Trump Presidency

Bill O'Neal

Sonoma Valley Press

Copyright © 2021 by William J. O'Neal
All rights Reserved

No part of this publication may be produced, stored in a retrieval system or transmitted in any form or by any means without the prior written permission of the copyright holder, except in excerpts used in a review. For permission information, write to Sonoma Valley Press, P.O. Box 1802, Sonoma, CA 95476

ISBN: 978-0-9828924-2-8

Published by
SONOMA VALLEY PRESS
P.O. Box 1802, Sonoma, CA 95476

Production and image editing by
Ona McLaughlin

Printed in the United States of America

This book is dedicated to my late wife, Dian Chevalier O'Neal, my best critic and life partner for 48 years. Thankfully, she lived to see the end of Donald the First's reign.

Table of Contents

Forward 1

2017: The Reign Begins 3

2018: From Russia with Love 35

2019: Midterm Hangover 67

2020: Pandemic Politics 97

2021: The Final Days 133

About Bill O'Neal 140

Forward

"All you need in this life is ignorance and confidence," Mark Twain once observed, "and then success is sure."

Bill O'Neal and Donald Trump have spent the last four years trying to prove Twain's point—one in the oval office and the other in editorial cartooning excellence.

That, however, is about the only thing O'Neal and POTUS 45 have in common, as the Bay Area humorist has made it his mission to document on a weekly basis the folly and corruption of Mr. Trump's stint as leader of the free world.

Since 2017 we've witnessed President Trump weaponize his reign with pettiness, prevarication and brash incompetence—while O'Neal has brandished a satirical sword smelt of ink, paper and a keen eye for the pathological to cut to the truth of the events of the day with Atticus Finch-like precision.

We'll have what O'Neal's having, thank you very much. We may still wake up the next morning with a MAGA-flavored hangover, but at least it tasted good going down.

When the histories of these unprecedented presidential years are written in the coming decades, many will target the chaos and chicaneries of our modern-day Lear-lite, but few will have done it with such a blend of whimsy, civil protest and outright personal indignation as Bill O'Neal.

Make no mistake, Twain was absolutely right And we've got a full four years of evidence from Bill and Donald to prove it.

May O'Neal's work these past few years stand the test of time. The other, not so much.

Jason Walsh
Editor & Associate Publisher
Sonoma Index-Tribune

2017
The Reign Begins

Devastated Democrats

Democrats are still shell-shocked from the 2016 election results, losing not only the White House, but both houses of Congress.

"What hit us?"

Jubilant Republicans

Republicans, on the other hand, are thrilled. The only branch of government they don't control is the judiciary, and they intend to remedy that soon.

"This is our town now!"

Inaugural Tweet

Anyone who thought Trump would cut down on tweeting once he became president is sadly mistaken. In fact, tweets become the signature of the Trump presidency.

"This is YUGE!
I'm being sworn in as President of the United States.
I am SO awesome!"

Inaugural Crowd

Trump claims to have attracted the largest crowd ever to attend an inauguration. The real crowd arrives a day later with the Women's March on Washington to protest Trump's election.

"Nobody can draw a crowd like me!"

Year of the Rooster

Trump's first year in office coincides with the Chinese year of the rooster, a perfect personification of Trump's cocky, boastful nature.

Government by Executive Order

Trump begins his presidency with a stream of executive orders. His most controversial order: a travel ban on seven Muslim countries, later struck down as unconstitutional.

"Another executive order for you to sign, Your Excellency!"

Killing Obamacare

One of Trump's major campaign pledges was to overturn the Affordable Care Act (Obamacare). Republicans immediately begin work on a new bill repealing the act.

"Trust us! This won't hurt a bit."

The Russian "Thing"

Meanwhile, Trump's connections to Russia and Vladimir Putin remain a mystery. Trump refuses to criticize Putin, even as the Russians step up their intervention in the Middle East.

"Donald, my friend, I have a great real estate redevelopment opportunity for you."

Putin's Puppet?

Does Putin have something on Trump? That's a question many Americans are asking, including the FBI as it investigates connections between Russia and the Trump campaign.

"What's going on here!?"

Trump Steps In It

Trump asks FBI Director James Comey to go easy on the bureau's investigation. When Comey refuses, Trump fires him. This triggers Trump's worst nightmare: appointment of an independent special counsel.

"Go easy on Flynn, big guy! We're all on the same team here!"

Die Obamacare, Die!

House Republicans pass a bill repealing the Affordable Care Act. The bill now goes to the Republican-controlled Senate, where it is expected to pass along party lines.

McCain to the Rescue

Republican Senator John McCain casts the deciding "no" vote as the Senate fails to pass the House bill repealing Obamacare. Trump is furious.

Conservative Win

But Trump does come though on another campaign promise. He fills the vacant Supreme Court seat with a conservative judge, Neil Gorsuch.

Trump White House

Trump describes his White House as a fine-tuned machine. In reality, it is a quarreling pack of back-biters, continually jockeying for political position.

Liar, Liar

Trump complains about his staff leaking inside information to reporters. In truth, it is frequently Trump himself who leaks things to the media.

"We need to find out where the fake news is coming from and put a stop to it!"

Revolving Door

Amid stories of White House dysfunction, Trump ousts Chief of Staff Reince Priebus and White House Press Secretary Sean Spicer. Director of Communications Anthony Scaramucci is then fired after only 10 days on the job.

"Hey, Sean, look who just walked in the door."

Perceived Disloyalty

Trump is mad at Attorney General Jeff Sessions for recusing himself from the Russia investigation. Only intervention by Republican senators keeps Trump from firing him.

"Get off, Sessions! We don't want weenies like you on this train!"

White Supremacy Apologist

"White nationalists" march through Charlottesville, Virginia, attacking protesters of Confederate statues. Trump plays down the clash, saying both groups included "some very fine people."

World's Worst Millennial

Trump and North Korean dictator Kim Jong-un begin an escalating exchange of insults over North Korea's testing of long-range missiles.

Glimpse of Armageddon

Trump threatens Kim with "fire and fury like the world has never seen" if North Korea continues its missile tests. The world takes a deep breath.

"What a loose cannon!"

Playing to His Base

Trump attacks NFL players who kneel during the national anthem to protest police violence against African Americans.

"*What losers! NFL players are such bad role models for America.*"

Going After Dreamers

In keeping with his anti-immigration stance, Trump ends DACA (Deferred Action for Childhood Arrivals), an Obama program protecting undocumented immigrants brought here as children.

"This sure beats going after REAL rapists and druglords!"

Horrific Hurricane Season

2017 is a hyperactive hurricane season—the costliest on record—with multiple Category 5 hurricanes, which cause extreme flooding along the Gulf and Florida coasts.

"*Still think climate change is a hoax, Donald?*"

Hurricane Maria

One of the worst hurricanes is Maria, which leaves half of Puerto Rico's population without power. Power outages last for months, but Trump still calls his administration's response "a fantastic job."

"Puerto Rico should be grateful for our fantastic relief response!"

Another Shot at Healthcare

Congressional Republicans try one more time to fulfill their campaign promise to repeal Obamacare. Once again, they fail.

"Use the siren! They'll get out of the way!"

The Big Tax Cut

Republicans have better luck with their other major campaign promise—a massive tax cut. The 2017 Tax Cut and Jobs Act doesn't get a single Democratic vote, but it passes anyway.

"*Trust us, sir, we won't rest until we've passed that tax cut you so richly deserve.*"

Billionaire Brotherhood

Trump signs the $1.5 billion tax cut into law on December 22. It's an early Christmas present for big corporations and wealthy donors. It also explodes the deficit.

"Love your tax cut, Mr. President."

Western Wall

Trump breaks with decades of U.S. policy by recognizing Jerusalem as the capital of Israel. Religious conservatives applaud.

*"You think this is something?
Wait'll you see the wall I'm building!"*

Congressional Complicity

Congressional Republican leadership continue to support Trump no matter what he says or does. They are happy to get their tax cut. No need to make waves.

See No Evil — MCCARTHY
Hear No Evil — MCCONNELL
Speak No Evil — RYAN

Independent Investigator

But there is one person who can possibly hold Trump accountable: Special Counsel Robert Mueller. As 2017 comes to a close, the nation waits to see whether Mueller's investigation will lead to impeachment.

"Don't worry! Mueller would never poke his nose in our family affairs!"

2018
From Russia with Love

Looming Shutdown

2018 begins with the threat of a government shutdown over a budget impasse. Funding crisis doesn't end until February 8.

God's Gift to Women

It comes to light that Trump's personal lawyer, Michael Cohen, paid adult film star Stormy Daniels $130,000 to keep quiet about her earlier tryst with Trump.

"Donny Baby!"

School Safety

Yet another horrendous school shooting takes place, this time in Parkland, Florida. Trump's solution to the crisis: arm school personnel.

"This is nothing! Try getting into Miss Chase's class!"

NRA Family Values

In the face of increasing calls for gun control, Trump continues to side with the NRA, going so far as to speak at the NRA national convention.

"*You can hit him, kid! You just need more firepower!*"

White House Turnover

Musical chairs at the White House continues. Secretary of State Rex Tillerson is the latest to be ousted, and dozens of other offices remain unfilled.

Duck and Cover

No one seems safe in Trump's White House, not even his own family. Chaos appears to be the order of the day.

"Just keep your head down until this blows over!"

Jumping Ship

Adding to White House problems, Speaker of the House Paul Ryan announces he will not seek reelection in November. It is seen as a repudiation of Trump.

"Where's Ryan?

Damage Control

Trump faces challenges from all directions—from nuclear threats from Iran and North Korea to Robert Mueller's Russia probe.

"This is exhausting!"

Tariff War

Trump launches a trade war with China, slapping tariffs on billions of dollars of Chinese products. Beijing retaliates by imposing tariffs on U.S. products such as soybeans and pork.

"You realize we are on the front lines of a global trade war!"

Iran Nuclear Deal

Keeping a campaign promise, Trump announces that the U.S. will withdraw from the Iran nuclear deal, leaving America's allies on their own.

"Hey! A little help here!"

Summit Expectations

Trump accepts an invitation from Kim Jong-un to meet. The summit finally takes place, but the only result is a vague proclamation pledging to work for a nuclear-free Korean Peninsula.

North Korean Deception

Kim's summit pledges prove to be empty promises. U.S. intelligence agencies report that North Korea continues to build nuclear missiles capable of hitting the U.S.

*"Excellent place to hide our nukes!
Trump never goes near places like this."*

Border Barbarities

To discourage illegal border crossing, U.S. immigration officials begin separating children from their parents as they try to enter the U.S.

"*You get the kids back when I get my wall!*"

Children in Cages

Children separated from their parents are held in cages at detention camps. U.S. courts order that the children be reunited with their parents, but poor record keeping makes this impossible for thousands of children.

"This is great! Nobody's talking about Russia now!"

Alternate Reality Goggles

Trump continues to dismiss Russian election interference as a hoax. Meanwhile, the Mueller probe indicts a dozen Russian intelligence officials for hacking Democratic Party emails.

"You're right, Mr. President. The Russians are our friends!"

The Putin Mystery

Trump and Putin meet in Helsinki for a one-on-one summit. Trump publicly accepts Putin's denial of Russian election interference, repudiating his own intelligence experts. People ask: what could Putin possibly have on Trump?

Real Witch Hunt

Trump begins dismissing the Mueller investigation as a witch hunt, vehemently denying his campaign ever colluded with the Russians to win the 2016 election.

Draining the Swamp

Members of Trump's inner circle begin to be sentenced as a result of the Mueller investigation, starting with Paul Manafort, Trump's campaign manager, and Michael Cohen, his personal lawyer.

Soiled EPA

Scott Pruitt, Trump's EPA administrator and enemy of environmental regulations, is forced to resign after multiple investigations into his management of the agency.

"I love this job!"

Another Supreme Court Win

Another Supreme Court seat opens up, and Trump nominates Brett Kavanaugh, a conservative. After a bruising Senate hearing filled with allegations of drunkenness, recklessness and sexual assault, Kavanaugh is finally confirmed.

"*Why, yesh, Senator, I do love beer! What's it to you?*"

Behind the Scenes

A bombshell book by political writer Bob Woodward is released. The book, based on numerous interviews with White House insiders, is highly critical of Trump's management style.

"I hope he fires YOU first!"

Trump's Loyal Supporters

Woodward's book doesn't seem to faze Trump's political base. This is good news for the GOP going into the 2018 midterm elections.

*"We don't care what the eggheads write about you.
We love you, man!"*

Environmental Denial

As wildfires sweep across the West Coast for the second year in a row, Trump continues to dismiss any link to climate change. His answer: do a better job of raking the forests.

*"I'll give you five minutes!
But it better not be more crap about climate change!"*

GOP Midterm Message

Trump is determined to make the congressional midterm elections about himself, even though he is not on the ballot. He is now the face of the Republican Party, for better or worse.

Hate and Fear

The political rhetoric of the midterms is even more vitriolic than 2016. The GOP appeals are largely based on fear and racism, a sneak preview of 2020.

"Van belongs to a Donald J Trump of Washington, DC."

Split Decision

In the midterms, Republicans increase their margin in the Senate but lose the House in a "blue wave." The GOP no longer has a monopoly on the levers of government.

"Ha! What Blue Wave?"

Acting Attorney General

Trump is finally able to get rid of Jeff Sessions. His replacement as acting attorney general is Matthew Whitaker, a critic of the Mueller probe.

"Watch your back with this new acting Attorney General!"

Christmas on the Border

Life remains grim for those trying to cross into the U.S. They are routinely tear-gassed, a practice Trump defends as "very safe."

Ghost of Watergate

Special Counsel Mueller's Russia investigation—and possible impeachment—loom over Trump as 2018 winds down. The media is full of comparisons with Watergate.

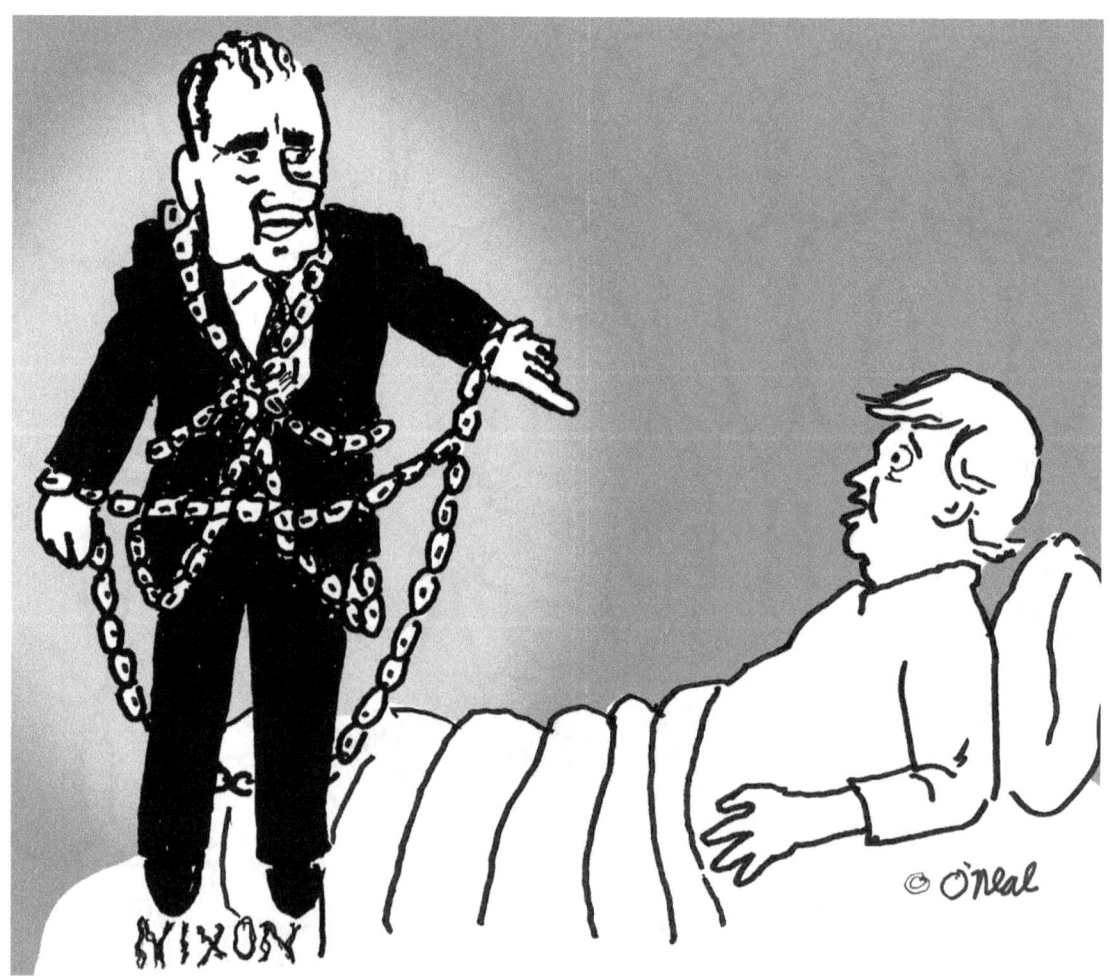

"I'm the ghost of previous Special Counsel investigations, and I'm here to warn you that if you have any tapes in your possession, destroy them now!"

Deja Vu

2018 ends as it began—with the government shut down. A partial government shutdown begins December 22, following failure of Congress and the administration to reach a funding compromise for Trump's border wall.

2019
Midterm Hangover

Still Shut Down

2019 begins with the government still in partial shutdown, as Trump battles Congress over funding for the border wall. It eventually becomes the longest government shutdown in U.S. history.

"Let them eat cake!"

Trump Tantrums

Trump's stalemate with Congress paralyzes the government. Trump finally blinks, and Congress passes a budget without funding for the border wall.

New Power Struggle

With Democrats now in control of the House, Trump's nemesis, Nancy Pelosi, is elected speaker of the House. Trump's political free ride is over

"Ha! Your lasso of truth doesn't phase me, Nancy!"

Another Trump-Kim Summit

Trump and Kim Jong-un meet again in another one-on-one summit. Despite gushing introductory remarks, the talks end early without any results.

Mueller Report Falls Flat

Special Counsel Robert Mueller submits his report on Russian interference in the 2016 election. Democrats are stunned to hear that it contains no charges of obstruction or collusion—the impeachable offenses they were looking for.

Trumpzilla Unchained

Before anyone outside the Justice Department can gain access to the report, Trump's new attorney general, Bill Barr, issues a four-page summary that absolves Trump of any impeachable offense. The summary ends up preempting the report itself.

Trump's Pet AG

Barr defiantly defends his actions to Congress. Trump finally has the Attorney General he wants, someone loyal to him personally rather than the country.

"*The president has been completely exonerated!*"

King and His Court

There seems to be little now to restrain Trump's authoritarian tendencies. His apparent desire is to rule without congressional interference—like a king.

The President's Men

Trump has escaped impeachment conviction, but thanks to the Mueller probe members of his inner circle—Paul Manafort, Mike Flynn, Michael Cohen—are in jail, and former Trump advisor Roger Stone is about to join them.

"Anybody heard from the Boss?"

Defending the Homeland

Meanwhile, events on the border are still chaotic. At the urging of White House aide Stephen Miller, Trump doubles down on the policies of child separation and detention camps.

"Judges next!"

Alternate Reality

Immigrant children separated from their parents continue to be held in detention camps—which Trump defends as improvements to their normal living situation.

"Look at this beautiful camp! These kids never had it so good!"

Real Americans

Trump puts Stephen Miller, an ardent nativist, in charge of immigration policy. Miller immediately expands deportation operations to residents not born in the U.S.

Tariffman

Trump boasts his tariff policies are winning the trade war with China. That's news to American farmers and manufacturers, who are getting killed by the Chinese tariffs.

"Hey, Mexico! You're next!"

Message from Kim

Trump and Kim Jong-un meet yet again. Like previous summits, this one accomplishes nothing. Kim continues to develop ever-more dangerous warheads and missiles.

"Kim Jong-un called. He has a surprise for you!"

Diplomatic Dabbling

During a 75th anniversary celebration of D-Day, Trump stops in to see Queen Elizabeth. The visit does little to reassure America's European allies about Trump's intentions.

Exit Without Honor

To the consternation of his military, Trump announces the withdrawal of the last U.S. special forces from Syria. The move leaves American allies the Kurds at the mercy of the Turks and Russians.

"It's all yours!"

Progressive Frontrunners

Meanwhile, on the home front, the race for the 2020 Democratic presidential nomination has begun. The progressive wing jumps off to an early lead.

"You sure this is the way to the White House?"

Growing Field

The number of Democratic presidential hopefuls quickly swells. All are running to the left in terms of proposed policies and programs.

Enter Biden

Former Vice President Joe Biden enters the race as a traditional centrist. He faces a daunting challenge given the progressive rhetoric of the other candidates.

"Sure you want to run that gauntlet, Joe?"

More the Merrier

The Democratic field continues to swell to more than 25 hopefuls. It takes two stages to accommodate all the candidates for the first debate.

"We're full up! You'll have to wait for the 2024 bus!"

Show of Disunity

The Democratic debates turn out to be brawls. No one emerges as the clear favorite.

The Trump Faithful

Meanwhile, Trump has begun his reelection campaign with his trademark rallies, filled with fanatic fans chanting their support. The battle is joined.

"Hillary was right! They really are deplorables."

Socialist Smear

Trump and his allies try to paint Democrats as dangerous socialists who will destroy the American dream—in contrast to Trump's call to "Make America Great Again."

Digging Up Dirt

Presuming Joe Biden will be his eventual opponent, Trump tries to dig up dirt on Biden's son, Hunter, for his business dealings in Ukraine. Trump puts Rudy Giuliani in charge of the effort.

"Hey, I may have found something here!"

Ukrainian Shakedown

Giuliani uses two Ukrainian associates, Lev Parnas and Igor Fruman, to squeeze information out of local officials. But there's no dirt to be had.

"Hey Boss, you got another job for us?"

Quid Pro Quo

Trump takes matters into his own hands during a phone call with Ukrainian President Volodymyr Zelensky. He urges Zelensky to open an investigation into Hunter Biden. In return, the U.S. will release aid money earmarked for Ukraine.

"First, you have to do me a favor!"

Impeachment Revisited

House Democrats jump on this as a chance to finally hold Trump accountable for his abuse of power. They launch a formal impeachment inquiry. Republican members do their best to discredit the proceedings.

Trump is Impeached

With only 13 days left in the year, the House impeaches Trump on charges of abuse of power and obstruction of justice. The vote is along party lines. It's now up to the Senate to decide Trump's fate.

"The peasants are here with a special gift, Your Highness."

2020
Pandemic Politics

Trump's Real Wall

Trump's Senate impeachment trial begins. Republicans believe they have the votes to control the outcome.

No Conviction

Republican senators refuse to consider new evidence or witnesses. The result is inevitable—Trump is acquitted.

"Behold the dark side of the Force!"

Meanwhile in Iowa

On the Democratic side, original presidential front-runner Joe Biden is fading.

"If I hang in long enough, I might just win this thing!"

Back from the Grave

But Joe Biden isn't finished. A huge win in South Carolina resurrects his campaign.

Hit and Run

Biden goes on to win 10 of the next 11 Democratic primaries. Sanders suspends his campaign.

"He came outta nowhere!"

Business as Usual

Meanwhile, Trump holds political rallies throughout January and February, dismissing repeated warnings of a deadly new virus sweeping the globe.

"Are you ready for four more years of this tremendous economy?"

Ignoring the Virus

Trump continues to downplay the new virus (it's just flu). Other than banning travel from China, his administration remains woefully unprepared for a major outbreak.

"*Stop being so dramatic! It's just a cold!*"

Grim Reality

By mid-March, the U.S. is in big trouble. Deaths are rising, the stock market is crashing and the nation faces shocking shortages of testing and medical supplies.

"*Who knew the virus could explode like this?*"

Mandatory Shutdowns

Trump passes the buck to the states to confront the virus Most governors close nonessential businesses and order residents to stay home. This shutdown, along with social distancing, is expected to blunt COVID-19's spread.

*"Change the channel one more time,
and you will end up in Intensive Care."*

Financial Safety Net

With most people out of work, Congress passes a series of relief bills, including one authorizing direct payment to millions of Americans.

Full-Fledged Pandemic

By April 30, the U.S. is the global epicenter of the pandemic. Thirty million Americans have lost their jobs, one million are infected and more than 65,000 have died, more U.S. deaths than due to the Vietnam War.

Reopening the Economy

Trump, who sees a revived economy as critical for his reelection, becomes the cheerleader for reopening the country despite the virus.

*"Here's you stimulus check.
Now get up and get this economy rolling again!"*

Virus be Damned

Even though the virus remains a huge threat, more and more governors begin to follow Trump's lead and reopen businesses without stringent precautions.

"Oh, yummy. It's party time!"

More Magical Thinking

Trump declares the pandemic practically over—even as new cases soar throughout the country. His administration even moves to end federal funding for coronavirus testing.

"Virus? What Virus?"

COVID Culture Wars

Wearing masks and social distancing become partisan symbols in the country's culture wars. Instead of trying to unite the country, Trump plays to his base by refusing to wear a mask

Attacking the Experts

Trump sees public health experts as obstacles to reopening the country. This includes the nation's leading expert, Dr. Anthony Fauci, who Trump now seeks to silence.

Back to School

With more than 43 million COVID-19 cases, the U.S. appears to be powerless to halt the virus. But that doesn't stop Trump from continuing to push for reopening schools and businesses

"Welcome back to school, kiddies. It will be such a treat!"

Double Trouble

The police killing of George Floyd in Minneapolis sets off massive protests across the country. The nation now faces two crises: the pandemic and the civil unrest over racial injustice.

Fanning the Flames

With the economy no longer a political asset, Trump sees a new path to reelection: exploit fear of potentially violent racial protests by championing law and order.

"*This has to be worth 2 million votes!*"

The Disinformation Twins

To nobody's surprise, Russia again tries to undermine U.S. elections. Ironically, the Russian disinformation campaign echoes Trump's own campaign against mail-in ballots and voter fraud.

Wrecking the Post Office

Convinced voting by mail favors the Democrats, Trump blocks emergency funding for the Postal Service. He also has his new Post Master General slow down the mail in order to cast doubt on postal delivery.

"That oughta slow 'em down!"

Republican National Convention

Trump uses the convention to rewrite the history of his administration, claiming the coronavirus has been conquered and the economy is back to pre-pandemic levels—in brazen defiance of facts.

"I AM THE GREAT AND POWERFUL **OZ**

CONQUEROR OF THE CORONAVIRUS PROTECTOR OF…

Hey, what's that dog doing?"

The Battle Is Joined

Democrats nominate Joe Biden and Kamala Harris to take on Trump and Pence. The final countdown to judgment day begins.

"Remember, this is a battle between the American Dream and Godless Socialism!"

Supreme Court Vacancy

Forty-five days before the election, Justice Ruth Bader Ginsburg dies, leaving a vacancy on the Supreme Court. Republicans rush to fill the seat with conservative justice Amy Comey Barrett before November 3rd.

Rose Garden Fiasco

Predictably, Trump's Rose Garden celebration of Amy Coney Barrett's Supreme Court nomination turns out to be a "super spreader" event. Multiple White House officials and senators come down with the coronavirus—including Donald Trump, who ends up in Walter Reed hospital.

Cult of Denial

After only four days, Trump leaves the hospital claiming to be cured. He goes back to pooh-poohing the virus, this time using his own "victory" over it to minimize the threat.

Election Night

King Donald is on full display. He and other Republican candidates surge to an early lead on strong "day-of" voting. Trump claims victory even though many votes still have to be counted.

Victory Begins to Slip Away

Vote by vote the tide turns as the results of mail-in ballots begin to mount. Trump screams fraud and calls on his legion of lawyers to stop the vote tabulation in key battle ground states.

"Unleash my lawyers! This vote-counting has to be stopped!

Trump Won't Concede

Four days later, news organizations call the election: 306 electoral votes for Biden, 226 for Trump. But Trump reuses to admit he lost, blocking any orderly transitions of administrations.

No Big Blue Wave

The election is much closer than Democrats had hoped for. Trump comes within 80,000 votes of repeating his 2016 electoral victory, and Republicans gain seats in the House and dominate state races. Control of the Senate rests on a January runoff election in Georgia.

Still No Concession

Trump continues to fight the election outcome. Crying fraud, he and his Republican allies launch a blizzard of lawsuits and political maneuvers to overturn the results in key swing states.

"We could invade Canada and invoke Martial Law!"

Clinging to Power

Lacking any evidence, all 50-plus GOP lawsuits are thrown out of court. The Electoral College makes it official by voting to confirm Biden's victory. But Trump still refuses to concede, clinging to the hope that Congress will refuse to certify the Electoral College vote in key states.

"It's not over! Congress can still stop this steal!"

Christmas Hope

Meanwhile, COVID-19 cases and deaths hit all-time highs. But hope has arrived. Two vaccines for coronavirus win FDA approval in December. Vaccinations begin Christmas week.

Still In Charge

As 2020 come to a close, Trump still retains all the powers of the presidency. What will he do with those awesome powers in his final days in office? This is a question on everybody's mind.

"You look like someone who could use a Royal Pardon!"

2021
The Final Days

Democrats Gain Control of Senate

The new year begins with a big Democratic win in Georgia. Democrats take both U.S. Senate seats in a special runoff election, breaking Mitch McConnell's grip on the Senate and the country.

"Don't let the door hit you on the way out!"

Last-Ditch Effort

The election is not official until both houses of Congress meet to count and certify the electoral college results. Trump exhorts his congressional allies to disrupt this process by objecting to the results from key states won by Biden.

"Now go forth and overturn those damned electoral results!"

Barbarians at the Gate

On the day of certification, Trump incites his followers to march on the Capitol and disrupt the proceedings. His supporters turn into a violent mob that storms the capitol building and rampages through the halls of Congress. The nation is appalled.

Clear and Present Danger

"What will Trump do next?" This is the question on everyone's mind in the final days of his reign. The House rushes to remove Trump from office, impeaching him a second time, just seven days before his term expires.

"How dare they call me unhinged!"

Capitol on Edge

Washington fears right-wing extremists will return to disrupt Biden's inauguration. The Capitol is turned into a Bagdad-like "Green Zone," with thousands of troops patrolling the streets.

"You aren't going anywhere until I see some ID!"

America Exhales

It's over! Biden and Harris are sworn into office. Donald the First's tumultuous reign comes to an end. Trumplicans everywhere mourn his exit; but the rest of the country heaves a sigh of relief.

About Bill O'Neal

Bill O'Neal has two major interests in his life: cartooning and politics.

He put the two together for the first time at the *Springfield Republican* newspaper in the 1960's. It was an amazing time filled with larger-than-life figures like JFK, LBJ and "Tricky Dick."

It was a great gig! But the pay sucked. A smart career path it was not.

So he went off to find his fame and fortune in the world of advertising.

Fast forward to 2008. O'Neal decides to leave Connecticut and join his wife in Sonoma, California. Eventually he's approached by the editor of the *Sonoma Index-Tribune*. "I understand you draw political cartoons," the editor says. "Would you be interested in drawing cartoons for us?"

Great opportunity, lousy pay! But this time O'Neal is in a different financial position. So he takes the gig. Just in time for the rise of Donald Trump.

"I thought Nixon was a great target for cartoonists," recalls O'Neal, "but Nixon was tame compared to Trump."

"Trump is everything our founding fathers warned us about," continues O'Neal, "totally self-serving, unprincipled, a would-be king. A clear and present danger to the Republic."

The past four years have proved the point. The cartoons and commentary in this book chronicle Trump's divisive, increasingly autocratic reign.

O'Neal's minimalist black-and-white cartoon style lends itself to telling the story. "I usually go for the humor in a situation," says O'Neal, "I don't get bogged down in the drawing; I do just enough to get the idea across."

"Historians are going to have a field day with Donald Trump," adds O'Neal, "but we should not wait for them to set the record straight. We need to do that now! That's the purpose of this book!"

Follow Bill O'Neal and his cartoons on:

beyondthepoliticalpale.com

Every week O'Neal posts a new cartoon and commentary on the site. While Donald Trump may not be his primary focus any longer, there are still plenty of politicians and people beyond the political pale.